~ i ~

AGAPHILEROS

"A"

Love the way it is supposed to be.

Author:

Roger A. Watson

ISBN: 098938960X
ISBN-13: 978-0989389600
All poems, sayings and Rogerisms written
by

Roger A. Watson.

Published by The Agaphileros Experience!

DEDICATION:

To Jessy; my inspiration, my teacher, my mentor, my best friend. There is not a day that goes by that I do not think about you. You may be gone but you have left a legacy of love in me. I promise to bring it to the world. The world will know what a great woman you were.

CONTENTS

ACKNOWLEDGEMENTS:

Thank you for buying this book.

For additional copies or booking info please contact us at: 206-279-1624.

Thanks to the women and men who helped me put this together. The ones who answered my questions and gave me insight. Who read and reread, edited and reedited. I thank you sincerely.

To the people who advised and supported me with purchases or with your presence. You are loved and I thank God for you.

To the real lovers out there who want to be better today than they were yesterday and better tomorrow than they were today; Love takes Work, requires Sacrifice and demands Change.

MOVEMENTS & DICTIONARY (D)

I have named the sections "Movements" (D) because I wanted to use a word more applicable than chapters because chapters are fixed. When you read a movement, it will be something that you have never seen before. A movement is a call to move; to go from one mind set to another. Movements cause adjustments. This book is not a story book, or a history book, or an autobiography. It is more of a workbook, a playbook and a text book all in one. "That is a Movement".

(D): Signifies that the word is defined and is a part of the "Dictionary" located in Movement 5.

INTRODUCTION:
What does it all mean?

Agaphileros (Ah-gah-fill-leh-ross) (D) means, "Love, the way it is supposed to be." I came up with "Agaphileros" by joining three Greek words; agape, phileo and eros. Agape is used to describe the love of God which is unconditional and advantageous, phileo is used to describe the love of brethren in the family of God, and eros is used to describe the intimate love between a man and a woman. Men, we often focus on eros which we soon discover is not enough to build a great relationship. Let me add that this book is by no means a theological lesson although theology is spread throughout the pages. You may ask me why I think that Agaphileros is love, the way it is supposed to be. Let me tell you a true story. In 1993, I married my best friend, Magdalene Jacinta

Jessy Isaac on the island of Trinidad. We faced many challenges, and most were my fault. However, by the time 1996 rolled in we were building a Championship Relationship.

What is a Championship Relationship (D)? It is a relationship wherein two people win every time, no matter what. Champions win even when they lose. Losing is just a hurdle on the way to the real finish line. Jessy and I won joy, peace, sexual satisfaction, and financial stability. Eventually, we won everything we touched. Winning does take some time. The love we had was the best of the best in my opinion. She never had to worry about me loving anyone else and neither did I have to worry about her loving someone else.

Allow me to give you some more information about us. In 2008, Jessy was diagnosed with lupus, then, after a few years of battling her illness she went on to be with the Lord in 2011. {I am writing a separate book to chronicle our life story and her final journey. It will be called, "Jessy: Love to the last breath."}We invested everything we had into each other. Furthermore, we got rid of the things that kept us from having a Championship Relationship and we brought in the things that helped us to win. We had a good life. We were not rich but we had enough. Her passing made me feel like all my life's investment was gone. I was devastated.

In October of 2012, the Lord spoke to me and said, "If you don't let go of the past, then I will not be able to give you the future I have for you." He then said, "Don't focus on her death. Focus on her life and the love that you both shared." I understood. I was delivered and I found a new passion for life.

We will explain more later on. Let us get into some words born from Agaphileros? An

Agaphileroso (D) is a man that walks in Agaphileros and an Agaphilerosa (D) is a lady that walks in Agaphileros. Yes ladies, you can learn also.

Some material may be unsuitable for children and if you are uncomfortable with romance, love and mushy feelings, be advised; you may encounter some of that. If you go on, know that you will be held responsible to be a lover. Use the tools of love that I will provide and enjoy the love, Agaphileros style.

MOVEMENT 1: WORK!

Agaphileros (Ah-gah-fill-eh-ross) has 3 main ingredients that make up its foundation: Work (D), Sacrifice (D) and Change (D). *Agaphileros takes Work, it requires Sacrifice and it demands Change.* That is how God gave it to me. You will hear these words a lot from me. Let me be frank with you, (although I'd rather be Roger with you), true love does have a cost, and that cost has to be paid by *two* people. Agaphileros is not a one person show. Agaphileros will not work if one person says yes and the other says maybe. When Jessy and I were arguing and fussing at each other, it hindered how we loved each other. When we heard about how true love gives the advantage, *we* had a revelation. That one series by Dr. Creflo Dollar gave *us* insight into true love. We will talk more about advantage later on in "Agaphileros B" and it will be a turning point in your relationship, if you understand it.

As we continue to lay the foundation it will become apparent that Agaphileros takes Work. Someone may say that since Agaphileros takes work I am going to work overtime on my job. Listen to me carefully. I am not talking about that kind of work right now. I am talking about the other kind of Work. No, not that one either, the other one. Let me explain before you confuse *me.* In 1996 we began our Agaphileros journey. Jessy and I were living on the campus of Atlanta Christian College, now called Point University. I was working full time and going to school. Our first beautiful daughter was already over a year old at this time. Our second beautiful daughter came later on. We had a conversation one day at our kitchen table where we came to the conclusion that failure was *not* going to be an option for our marriage. We knew that we loved each other, and we were convinced that we could recapture that love. So the first thing we did was go back to Work. Listen, Work is doing the *simple things* to the best of your ability and doing it all the time.

Work for us was writing out a declaration about what we wanted so we could say it together, and when we were apart from each other. It was praying together. It was planning fun things to do. It was me opening every door every single time. It was us going the extra mile to keep each other happy. It was me helping out more with the baby so that we could get to church on time rather than fussing at her about being late. It was me taking better care of myself. Hello men! For me it was practicing better hygiene, seeing the dentist and the doctor when necessary, cleaning up after myself, (even your mother does not want to pick up after you), not talking when my mouth was full of food, doing a proper intestinal cleanse to ease up the smell in the toilet. It was her remembering which meals I loved and cooking them more often. It was me spending less time with the 'boys' and more time with my best friend. It was picking up an extra shift on the job when possible so that I could afford to buy her something special. It was us celebrating every anniversary and accomplishment. It was talking about everything, and I mean everything. I have learned so much about women just from talking to my wife and raising 2 girls. I still have a lot to learn though.

What can you work on to make your relationship a better one? I have the answer for you. It's YOU. Work on yourself. I didn't tell Jessy what to cook unless she insisted. I didn't ask her to memorize which meals I liked and cook them more often. She didn't tell me to come right home after work. She didn't tell me to surprise her with a special gift. She didn't tell me to be a better conversationalist. I never asked *her* to become better. I simply told her that *I was going to be better*. One of my mottos is this; "I will be better today than I was yesterday and I will be better tomorrow than I am today." Can you stand to be a better person? How about a better lover? Maybe a better listener? Maybe a better responder? Jessy always told me that she was a "responder". Responder to what you ask? My desires. So do you know what I did? I became a responder to her desires too. Men, the first responder gets fed after he does the Work.

Let me add this point. The shortest distance between two points is the right way. Most of us have been taught how to love by the standards of the world. I believe that we should be willing to be taught by the creator of love who is God. He knows the right way. The first thing that we see God doing in the Bible is Working. In the Amplified Bible it says in Genesis 1:1, **"In the beginning God (prepared,**

formed, fashioned, and) created the heavens and the earth." (I broke a sweat just thinking about all that work). In the Ten Commandments God instructed His people to labor or work for six days and rest on the seventh day, which He called the Sabbath. As a matter of fact, the implication is that His people should labor *and* do all their work for six days straight, sun up to sun down. Dear friend, have you really been Working on the relationship you have for six days straight? Let me see your hands if you have. Good for you. As for the rest of us special people, we know we have not. I confess to you that I did not always Work for six days straight on my relationship with Jessy, but I did Work every day on it. In the Gospel of John 5:17 (CEB) Jesus told some people that His Father had been working even until then and that He has never ceased working. He is still working even to today. Understand this; loving someone like God requires you to love them will require Work. I was not in bondage to a Law or the commandments, I was free to live in Grace and so are you. I chose to Work on my relationship voluntarily and God honored that. Friends, I was working on the shortest distance to true love; the right way. What are you working on?

Know this, whatever you want to happen for yourself, make it happen for someone else and God can make it happen for you. In life you reap what you sow, just not in the same quantity. The quality is the same but not the quantity. You don't plant an apple seed and get one apple do you? No, you get an apple tree with an abundance of apples. I want you to know, anything that is successful will take some Work. Nothing good comes easily. My friend Brian often says that a Chinese man told him, "Good ting no cheap and cheap ting no good." (Source unknown). Your effort for an inter-personal relationship must equal your expectation for that inter-personal relationship. If you want a Championship Relationship then you have to calculate what Work will be required to get it.

The operative question will be this, "Do you want a Championship Relationship?" Since you picked up this book, maybe you are considering it. Good decision! I believe that you are on your way to becoming an Agaphileroso or an Agaphilerosa. If you want it bad enough, you will do the Work. So roll up your sleeves, it's time to get to Work!

WHAT CAN YOU WORK ON?

- Your spirit. Spend some time with God. He is not bad at all and He listens well. You can tell Him anything, really. He wants to help all of us (and you know we need help; lots of help).

- Your attitude. Work on just being nicer.

- Your way of thinking. Trust me; you will need to renew your mind to Agaphileros constantly.

- Your forgiveness and mercy levels. Work on raising them to *instant level* instead of *later level*. Stop 'holding' people. Release them from your heart.

- Your communication skills. *If you don't have any, you can buy them on sale at Wal-Mart.* Just kidding. Work on making people glad that they are listening to you. Listen and respond Agaphileros style.

- Your selfishness. Work on becoming selfless.

- Your bad habits. *"Well that is just how God made me."* Liar. Oops. Work on getting rid of those irritating issues that NOBODY likes. Really, they don't. God made you to become like Jesus not stay the way you are. That was a song by Billy Joel not by God.

- Your hygiene. Yes, the odor can be removed for the most part. Other people have to live in the house too. Please work on that.

- Your handling of money. Work on reducing waste, (not the one from your hygiene).

- Your health. Rest, Exercise, Nutrition. Put down the donut and step away from the table. Yes you. And go to bed! Yes me.

- Your caring and attentiveness. Work on paying attention to the other person and sincerely care about their well being and happiness.

- Your joy. Be happy, a lot. It's good for you because it makes you feel good about life. And stop being mad so often. You will cause your blood pressure to rise and hurt your body. Not to mention you will hurt the people you love by being angry.

- Your balance. Work on being a balanced individual. Spirit, soul and body.

MAKE YOUR OWN LIST OF THINGS TO WORK ON:

_____

_____

_____

_____

_____

_____

_____

_____

TAKE-AWAYS

- Agaphileros has 3 main ingredients that make up its foundation: Work, Sacrifice and Change. Agaphileros takes Work, it requires Sacrifice and it demands Change.

- True love does have a cost, and that cost has to be paid by *two* people. Agaphileros is not a one person show. Agaphileros will not work if one person says yes and the other says maybe.

- What can you work on to make your relationship a better one? I have the answer for you. It's YOU. Work on yourself.

- Be better today than you were yesterday and be better tomorrow than you are today.

- Learn to respond to each other's desires.

- The shortest distance between two points is the right way. The shortest distance to true love is the right way.

- In life you reap what you sow, just not in the same quantity. The quality is the same but not the quantity.

A PRAYER FOR WORK

Father, _____ and _____ (we) come to You today thanking You for all that You have done for us. Even as we enter into this time of Work we ask that You will open our eyes to understand love even better than we did before. It is our desire to know love the way You intended it to be and to do the Work required in order for us to be successful. So we begin with prayer. We want to Work for You and Work for each other in love. Show us the work that we must do in order to make our relationship a Championship Relationship. We ask You to spoil all the plans of our enemies domestic and foreign, seen and unseen, visible or invisible, and grant us great success in Agaphileros. We live under an open heaven of blessings and no weapon formed against this union will destroy what we have built. We are truly blessed. Anoint us for the Work that is ahead and equip us with all the necessary tools that we will need to effectively establish true love between us. We believe You for the victory every moment of every day for the rest of our lives and claim a successful journey ahead, in Jesus name, Amen.

DECLARATION FOR WORK

We declare and believe today that we are blessed to be a blessing and the blessing remains on our home. We declare and believe today that if God be for us then no one can defeat us. All of our enemies are cut down and the Lord is giving us the victory every day. We declare and believe that greater is He that is in us and in this relationship than he that is in the world outside of this relationship. We speak blessings over our Work time, our intimate time, our away time, our finances, our family, our friends and their relationships. We speak blessings over our bodies and declare that they are ready for anything because we take good care of our bodies. We declare that we eat the right things at the right time for health. We declare that we exercise when necessary and when possible so that we can be ready for whatever whatever. We speak blessings over our minds and declare that we are not filled with fear or jealousy, anger or insecurities. We think right thoughts and not wrong thoughts. We control ourselves and our emotions and will have no emotional failures. We have the right emotions to fully grasp and establish Agaphileros at all times and we will work until the job is done. We declare and believe that our spirits are right before God and we are not deliberately making it difficult for God to bless us. We are easy to bless because our heart is right before God and we are full of His grace. We declare and believe today that we pursue the passion necessary to be happy with each other at all times and we will not faint or give up or quit trying to be the best at loving each other. We are champions of love and we win every time. Love never fails so we declare that we never fail where our love is concerned. I declare and believe that we will love each other forever.

Notes: What do you like about your lover?

1. _____

2. _____

3. _____

4. _____

5. _____

6. _____

7. _____

8. _____

PERMANENT PURPOSE vs. TEMPORARY PLEASURES & TEMPORARY PURPOSE

Never give up a Permanent Purpose (D) for a Temporary Pleasure (D) or for a Temporary Purpose (D). If you step out of what is permanent into what is temporary, you will not have the best relationship that you can have. That is why you need protection from Temporary Pleasures and Temporary Purposes. So if God has blessed you with a Permanent Purpose surely He will bless you with a Permanent Protection Package from Temporary Pleasures and Temporary Purposes. The Protection Package is built in to the Permanent Purpose. If you step out of the Purpose you step out of the Protection Plan.

What is a Permanent Purpose? It is when God has given you the plans that He has for you and they will not change. This includes career, business, and yes spouse. For example, as I am writing this to you I know that I have a Permanent Purpose that involves writing books, holding "Agaphileros Experiences" and reaching out to people about relationships. That is my Permanent Purpose which means that it will not change. A Temporary Pleasure might be opening a Landscaping company. This may get me into what is temporary and cause me to neglect what is permanent. To make the point more poignant, what if God blesses you with Purpose, and someone who is everything that you need and want at the same time? He or she is it! And as you are building this wonderful relationship, some other person comes into your life who likes you a lot. What if they were sexually attracted to you? One of two things can happen. You will say no and keep on building, or you will say yes and stop building. When you say yes to what is temporary, you say no to what is permanent.

I remember having moments between the time I left Trinidad and the time Jessy actually arrived in Atlanta. It was 5 years, 6 months and 2 ½ weeks. During that time, I had a lot of opportunities to go after things that were not permanent. I will be careful to relate the following so that no one is hurt. There were a few notable temporaries. (The names were changed to protect the innocent). Please do not ask me about these when you see me because I will not reveal anymore than what you have read.

Shirley was one and she was a person that was from another country that I had felt a great connection towards. I was ready to give up everything permanent to pursue this younger woman until one day the Lord allowed me to see her with someone else. This was literally a day after we were intimate together. Temporary.

Matilda was another lady who was younger with 2 kids. I went by her house one day and I contracted chicken pox from one of her kids. Isn't that a shame? That was the end of that. Temporary.

Shaqueeda was the last one and she was married, older and had a couple of kids. As T.D. Jakes indicated, it is easier to get someone who has been worked on than to get a new one that needs a lot of work. (There are so many ways to interpret that statement). Hence the reason that married people is so "attractive". That did not go well because the husband figured out that we were talking to each other too much and he assaulted me. Yes, that was one of the fights I lost. Actually, I have lost both fights that I have been in. I don't even know why I show up to a fist fight. Temporary.

I said all of that to say that there were Temporaries that showed up, but at the end of the day, all I needed was already given to me on Day 1.

As a matter of fact, my Permanent Purpose was waiting in Trinidad while I was learning the difference between permanent and temporary, literally getting my head knocked around. Jessy did not have anyone to beat me up (thank God), and in addition, she was the one that God told me that He had chosen for me.

Agaphilerosos, be very afraid of Temporaries. Solomon talks about the lure of the strange woman in Proverbs 5:3-14. He was not joking. But thank God He always gives an alternative to Temporaries. Proverbs 5:15-19 gives instruction for men to seek the Permanents. I like the part that says that you should allow her breasts to satisfy you at all times and be ravished with her love. Yes sir! There is nothing wrong with that statement and nothing wrong with Permanent breasts, and all the Agaphilerosos said, "Amen!"

I know that we are talking about Purpose, but your relationships are the biggest part of your Purpose. Choose your mate well because they will help you get to your Purpose or keep you from it. We also know that today infidelity is common in marriage. So is abuse, lack of commitment, uncaring attitudes, and more. In the Gospel of Matthew 25:12, the Bible says that the love of many people will become cold. It is a sign of the end of this age. We must develop a better and warmer way; love.

How do you find out what your purpose is? I'm glad you asked. Let me say this, I believe that your Purpose can be found in your T.A.G.S.; Talents, Abilities, Gifts and Skills. I'll tell you why. God places certain desires in you. These T.A.G.S.s, as I call them, will be the things that most excite you because they will be the things that you are most proficient in doing. These are the things that you can do without necessarily getting monetary compensation. It is easy for you like writing is easy for me. I can write without stopping to eat. I could write for fun and for free (but I still want you to buy the books though).When you discover your T.A.G.S. you can make a career, a business or an organization out of them and receive compensation for what you love. For example, God will not give you a love of water and then send you someone who loves the desert. You will find yourself hanging around water and people who love water.

Another analogy that I use is this. If your Purpose is in California and you are leaving from Georgia, then you have to travel west to get to your Purpose. It is conceivable that you will meet many people on your way. Some may be from Georgia and may decide to travel with you. However, they may only go as far as Alabama. A person whose goal is Alabama is not your mate. Even if someone says that they will go with you until you get to Texas. They are not your mate. You need someone going to the same destination as yourself. Why would God give you someone that will hinder your Purpose? He won't. What happens many times is that we fall in love and forget to ask all the right questions and make all the right moves.

Ask questions. She's fine and all, but does she want any kids? He looks like he is built for anything, but does he have plans to make a living? Maybe in Agaphileros B we will give you a questionnaire of the things that you should ask before you say "I do". Sir, seek God for the reason that you were born before you marry a wife. Ladies, you need to seek God for your Purpose before you seek Him for an Agaphileroso. Know thyself before you try to know someone else. That way you will already know your destination and will not be deceived by someone going in the wrong direction.

I can hear some of you asking, "What if I am already married and now my spouse and I are heading to opposite Purposes. We want out but are so ashamed or will be so embarrassed. Many people were expecting us to make it but we just cannot." Or maybe one of you is being abused or the other party has no interest in building a Championship Relationship? Whatever the reason, you realize that you cannot build with what you have at this time. This is a good time for me to interject that I am not your official counselor and I do suggest that you sit down with one, if you can. I also recommend having a multitude of good counselors. Pick your counselors well. If Cousin Joe has been married 15 times and going through another divorce, he is probably not the best person to give you marital advice. However, although he may not be able to tell you what to do, you can learn some of what not to do from him. See what he does and don't do it! Find people that have a Championship Relationship and ask questions.

If all else fails and you have to get a divorce, know that God hates divorce but He will always love divorcees because God loves people. In Malachi 2:15-16 the Bible talks about how a man should not cheat on his wife because God hates divorce. It also says that God hates the man who commits violence against his wife. These are the faults of a man. He does not mention anything about the woman getting a divorce until the New Testament. (We will develop the Divorce matter in "Agaphileros B.") So we must be careful not to take this verse out of context when speaking to a woman. This is not her verse.

When a person has to walk away to save their life, their kids or their Purpose, I would not stop them. That is not my job. My job is to love you and tell you that you can find true love in the earth while building a Championship Relationship with someone. My job is to tell you that God wants you happy and He will not change His mind about that, ever. My job is to tell you that you should seek your Purpose because it is the most important thing you must have when you begin to build a Championship Relationship. My job is to tell you not to die without fulfilling your Purpose. My job will never be to beat you upside your head with my books while someone else is beating you up with their fists, their mouth and their actions. I have seen too many good women destroyed by wicked men for me to beat you down in a book.

On the contrary, what I will advise both Agaphilerosos and Agaphilerosas to do is spend some time with God and seek Him about your Purpose. Find what Permanent is for you and then pursue it. Because if you don't know what Permanent is then you may not know when

Temporary shows up. The most common relationship error today is people taking Temporary things and trying to fit them into Permanent positions. I do not think that most people know what their God-given Purpose is. Ask five people tomorrow and see what they say.

So I will conclude by encouraging you. Do not let the pain of the past keep you from the promise of the future. The best is yet to come for you. God has it all planned and He can see the bigger picture. Trust His judgment for your life. No one can do a better job with your future than He can. That is what I believe.

What do you think your Permanent Purpose is?

- _____

_____

_____

_____

What are some Temporaries in your life?

- _____
- _____
- _____
- _____
- _____
- _____
- _____
- _____
- _____
- _____

TAKE-AWAYS

- Your Purpose is within your T.A.G.S.s.

- Your Purpose is one of the most valuable items that you can take into a marriage.

- Never give up a Permanent Purpose to go after Temporary Pleasures or Temporary Purposes.

- What is a Permanent Purpose? It is when God has given you the plans that He has for you and they can include career, business, and spouse.

- When you say yes to what is temporary, you say no to what is permanent.

- Your relationships are the biggest part of your Purpose so choose your mate well because they will help you get to your Purpose or keep you from it.

- Many times we fall in love and forget to ask all the right questions and make all the right moves.

- Sir, seek God for the reason that you were born before you marry a wife. Ladies, you need to seek God for your Purpose before you seek Him for an Agaphileroso. Know thyself before you try to know someone else.

- If you don't know what *Permanent* is then you may not know when *Temporary* shows up. The most common relationship error today is people taking Temporary things and trying to fit them into Permanent positions.

- Do not let the pain of the past keep you from the promise of the future. The best is yet to come for you.

- Remember California.

- Temporaries are coming. Beware.

NOTES AND REMINDERS

MOVEMENT 2: SACRIFICE!

Sacrifice is the second essential ingredient to success in the arena of Agaphileros. I am not talking about cutting off a body part or disfiguring yourself for your lover. I am talking about the price you will have to pay. It can be literal or figurative. When Jessy and I were building what we had, I had to go to a dance class, I had to learn patience, I had to learn about taking care of babies, I had to give up on some plans of mine, I had to give up on some preconceived ideas about what a man should or should not be willing to do, I had to learn about money, I had to become more serious about God, I had to take extra time to groom myself, and the list goes on. These were Sacrifices to me. They cost something, but cost is irrelevant when Purpose (a Championship Relationship) is at stake. Sacrifice can be costly, but it also has great rewards. Most importantly I had to be prepared to Sacrifice whatever for the team. All successful teams pay a price to win; the owner(s), the coaches, the players, the staff and the fans. Some will have to sacrifice their time, others their resources and some will have to sacrifice their energy. They all have to play their part for the Championship.

In Agaphileros, Sacrifice begins when you *desire* to be successful in your relationship. However, I believe that something has to trigger your desire to win where your relationships are concerned. Something has to convince you that the Championship is worth the price you will have to pay and the Sacrifices that will be required. Some of you already had the desire triggered by a past experience; good or bad. Maybe you saw your parents create a wreck of a relationship. Maybe one of them had an affair. On the other hand maybe you saw grandma and grandpa love each other to the very last breath. Or maybe it was your best friend's parents that were always affectionate with each other. Maybe it was a relationship that you ended and the person you should have been with ended up in the arms of someone else. Whatever or whoever it was, it would have triggered the desire for a successful relationship in you. The fire has been lit and now you want better.

My trigger was two-fold; first, seeing my parents go through a rough marriage that ended in divorce and second, ending a relationship that I should not have ended. I could not have done anything about the first one, but as far as the second trigger was concerned, I made sure that when the next great woman (Jessy) came into my life I did what I was supposed to do so that we could win, together. Do you want to be better or do you want to improve the relationship that you already have? Then do it. Let us become better together. If your desire has been triggered, then get ready to make the necessary Sacrifices to be the best lover that you can be.

Elton John sang a song called; "Sacrifice" and he said that it was no sacrifice at all actually. Trust me in this when I tell you, when you have found the "one" like I did, the things that you will have to Sacrifice will seem like nothing because of Agaphileros. Jesus went to an old rugged cross, suffered and died for us, and his Sacrifice was the perfect example for us to see what Sacrifice is all about. Think about it... has anyone ever paid a greater price? I don't think so. He never stopped the process of Sacrifice even when He saw the cost. Why? He was thinking about you, the church and what you would need to be successful. In addition, the Bible says, **"As for husbands, love your wives, just like Christ loved the church and gave himself for her."** (The CEB, Ephesians 5:25). It sounds sacrificial for the man and that is how it should be. We as men should be willing to bear the brunt of the responsibility to build a Championship Relationship. No, I am not letting women off the hook, but they are designed by God to be responders to men who handle responsibility. At least, that is what I think. Do you want to see a relationship go from underperforming to average performing to over performing? Most of the time when a man makes the necessary Sacrifices things will change. This is an adult book so I can be a bit real at times and put away the sugar coating.

Let me talk briefly about some of the things I had to sacrifice. Before Jessy and I got married, the basis of my sex education was garnered, many years before, on the streets of Trinidad through friends, family members and the porn movies that I saw. Needless to say, getting an education like that created a warped view of sex. As a matter of fact, I was bewildered as to how to bring Jessy to an orgasm, (it is a good thing that she can't read this. I would probably be on silent treatment for a decade). It literally took me some weeks and "I" had sex often. I said "I" because I was getting most of the pleasure. But to my brothers let me say this, there is nothing like bringing your woman to an orgasm or multiple orgasms. (And all the women said, Aaaamen!) After a few deep conversations and gaining some understanding of how a woman's body works, progress! You know that the big "O" does not mean Oprah right? No buddy. It's that first *orgasm* that she experiences with you.

Jessy was a great teacher and she was patient. Take note ladies. She was patient. Don't destroy your man by emasculating (D) him. She could have done that to me but she decided instead to educate me. Choose education over emasculation. I was a decent student and a very determined husband. Take note men. I humbled myself. I was willing to Sacrifice my ego (D) to gain a Championship.

Also, do not be afraid to Sacrifice your mind-set: your education, experiences and influence. These make up your mind-set (D) or how you set your mind. Your education comes from a teacher in some formal setting. Your experiences come from life's journey. Your influences are those people and things that can impact your decision making process. As a matter of fact, these three areas make a great impact on any Championship Relationship. I only started with the sex part because most of you are thinking about getting some or are unsatisfied because you haven't gotten any lately or are wishing that your spouse would get a clue. Lol. (Can you say lol in a book?)

Sacrifice your miseducation. I tell women this often, if a man is teachable he's keepable. I also tell men all the time to sit at the feet of their woman and ask them, "Baby, how do you want me to love you?" If he is humble enough to ask that question and respond with action, you may have yourself an Agaphileroso. A word of caution to my Agaphilerosas. If a man will not learn before he says "I do", the odds are pretty good that he will not learn after he says "I do". He may not want to Sacrifice his education for you. On rare occasions men get a clue *after* saying I do, but for the most part we will be who we are long after we say I do. It is because of the mind-set; education, experience and influence. We can also be miseducated in the church as learned men of theology tell us what they think a man should do and what the role of a woman should be. Some relish in saying that a woman should be submissive and they use Ephesians 5:22 for emphasis, forgetting that the verse right before it talks about how both the husband and the wife should submit to one another in the fear of God (verse 21). And then verse 23 puts the heavier burden for the relationship upon the shoulders of the man. He has to be willing to Sacrifice his *life* for her, literally. (How you like me now?)

Sacrifice your experiences. What I learned on the streets and in a movie was not the best reality. I needed to get rid of that junk and learn something else. There was this guy who lived in the area where I grew up that beat his woman almost every weekend when they both got drunk. They called him, "Sweet man". Sad. He was not a man at all but a beast. I have also heard some people say that men from the "islands" think that it is ok to hit their women for whatever reason. I sure hope that mentality is not true or at least changing because that is a behavior that must stop. As boys, we grew up hearing and seeing women beaten and abused.

Some took that experience and did the same thing. I never hit Jessy and I am pretty sure if I did I would not have hands today. I lost my two fights remember, and she won all of hers. That would have been my last fight. I would have retired hands free. (My nickname would be hands free or blue tooth.)

On a serious note to all men everywhere, not just from the "islands", I spoke of violence against women as an example because it happens. But whatever experiences life has brought to you or is bringing to you that are a liability for a Championship Relationship, I beg of you to Sacrifice it today. God can help you with it or contact my office and I will get you in touch with the right resource. You can also contact your local pastor or resource facility for help. Don't be less than a man.

Agaphilerosas, if what you experienced has convinced you that trapping and manipulating men is right, Sacrifice it today. Whatever you trap or cage will eventually want its freedom. Maybe you cannot trust a man because of your past experiences with men. Maybe you saw your mom or sister or friend abused and ruined by a beast of a man. (Not a real man. *A real man will never ruin a good woman*). Do not treat your Agaphileroso like he is a beast. I know it is a hard thing for you because women are designed to contain and retain things and you contain and retain well, too well sometimes. Remember Nehemiah 12:43 (CEB) ***"They offered great sacrifices on that day and rejoiced, for God hath made them rejoice with great joy. The women and children also rejoiced, and the sound of the joy in Jerusalem could be heard from far away."*** When there was Sacrificing it produced rejoicing. So if Sacrificing produced rejoicing, is it possible that great Sacrificing can produce great rejoicing? You need to find out. An

Agaphileroso will make you rejoice, I guarantee it. Let your rejoicing be heard in this nation and around the world. Let your children see a Championship Relationship and rejoice. Sacrifice that experience that is *inside* so that you may become the happiest woman *inside* and *outside.* It's worth it.

Sacrifice your influences. Yes, a man should leave his "influences" and cleave only to his wife. Remember, she is supposed to be your best friend. Genesis 2:24-25 (CEB) *"This is the reason that a man leaves his father and mother and embraces his wife, and they become one flesh. The two of them were naked, the man and his wife, but they weren't embarrassed."* The man will have to leave his greatest influences and join with his wife to become one new person. It did not say leave God because He stands above this statement. Neither is it implying that you cannot have good counselors, trusted friends and expert advice from family members and others. To me, it is implying Movement. Moving from one status to another. Sacrificing the old so that the new can grow the right way. When the devil came and influenced Eve, she began to move away from success. When Eve took that influence and brought it to Adam, Adam now had a choice: Sacrifice the influence or take it and apply it. He should have cut it off right then and there. Notice, the man held the key to stopping the negative outside influence. They did not sin until he took the negative influence and applied it. I have nothing against in-laws, against friends or against family members. I have great in-laws, friends and family members, but the bottom line is this. If there is anyone or anything influencing you more than God and the person you are becoming one with, look out, an accident may be pending. Jessy and I had conversations so that we could gain a new and better understanding of oneness. I knew that I loved her more than anyone in the whole wide world and I was going to do whatever was needed to make her happy. I Sacrificed all other influences and clung to her. She did the same and then we became one. God joins Agaphilerosos and Agaphilerosas because He wants to have the final word and the final move between both of them. This is how He gets the glory. Remember, you are building a new person; the two are becoming one brand new person.

Let me also add that Adam and Eve were not embarrassed, even though they were naked. When I read that I thought about this. Jessy told me some things that are going to the grave with me and I told her some things that she took to her grave. We were naked before each other. When you are experiencing Agaphileros you have to Sacrifice the precious things for each other; those private memories. Tell the other person everything that you can so that there will be no surprises later on, no embarrassments. Become "naked" before your mate.

Agaphilerosos, do you still love your wife? Are you willing to Sacrifice whatever is necessary? There is hope for your relationship. Ask her to tell you how to love her, and then do it. Ask her what she doesn't like and then stop doing it. Do the good, stop the bad and enjoy the benefits.

Agaphilerosas, do you still want your marriage to work? Talk to him. Find out what he needs from you and do it. Count the cost; is it worth going into the relationship at a deeper level? Reality Check. Do not focus on the wedding so much that you miss the Sacrifices that will be needed for the marriage to succeed.

And finally my brethren, (I've always wanted to say that so I can sound like the Apostle Paul), be willing to make physical, mental, emotional and spiritual Sacrifices in order to build a Championship Relationship.

One of the greatest Sacrifices that I have ever had to make was letting Jessy go. She literally had to show up in a dream and tell me to let her go on that fateful Monday morning. Ultimately, she wanted to be in a better place and I was holding her back with my selfish prayers and my selfish faith. I was wrong. I know now that you should always seek your lover's best interests even if it cost you yours. She spent years sacrificing for her family and I almost messed up her journey because of my selfishness. That Monday was twenty days from her request to be taken off the machine and sixteen days in her final comatose state. That day I spoke to her in her ear and told her that she could go, and then she died. Selah.

I know this one thing. No Sacrifice seems enjoyable at the time, but when I think of her meeting Jesus, her dad and so many others she knew, I feel good. I made a Sacrifice that she wanted and needed from me. She is now having the advantage and that is the way that it should be. Find out what your lover needs from you and give it to them. That is Agaphileros.

WHAT CAN YOU SACRIFICE?

- TIME. One of three main commodities that you have and probably the most important one. The other two are resources and energy. You cannot be successful without sacrificing your Time. Everything you do has Time attached to it, everything. We will discuss more about Time and the other commodities in "Agaphileros B."

- RESOURCES. If you have it you must be willing to sacrifice it. Do not hold back from your lover. They need it. One thing that a real lover cannot stomach is a cheap person.

- ENERGY. Burn baby burn. Agaphileros needs a lot of energy to be sacrificed. But the benefit is that you get energy back. Remember, you reap commodities that you sow.

- MIND-SET. If it isn't right, get rid of it. What you thought was true years ago may now be false. Trust God to give the final word on a matter and He will make the final move in your situation.

TAKE-AWAYS

- Sacrifice can be costly, but it also has great rewards.

- Cost is irrelevant when Purpose is at stake.

- All successful teams pay a price to win; the owner(s), the coaches, the players, the staff and the fans. They all have to play their part for the Championship.

- In Agaphileros, Sacrifice begins when you *desire* to be successful in your relationship.

- Do you want to see a relationship go from underperforming to average performing to over performing? Most of the time it will be because of a man who makes the necessary sacrifices.

- Don't destroy your man by emasculating him. ***Educate don't emasculate.***

- Education, Experiences and Influence have a great impact on Championship Relationships.

- If a man is teachable then he is keepable.

- The heavier burden for the relationship is upon the shoulders of the man. He has to be willing to Sacrifice his *life* for her, literally.

- Whatever experience life has brought to you or is bringing to you that may be a liability for a Championship Relationship, I beg of you to Sacrifice it today.

- Agaphilerosas, if what you have experienced has convinced you that trapping and manipulating men is right, Sacrifice it today. Whatever you trap or cage will eventually want its freedom.

- A real man will never ruin a good woman.

- When there was Sacrificing it produced rejoicing. An Agaphileroso will make you rejoice, I guarantee it. Let your children see a Championship Relationship and rejoice.

- Sacrifice that experience that is *inside* so that you may become the happiest woman *inside* and *outside.*

- If there is anyone or anything influencing you more than God and the person you are becoming one with, look out, an accident may be pending.

- God joins Agaphilerosos and Agaphilerosas because He wants to have the final word and the final move between both of them. This is how He gets the glory.

- Agaphilerosos, do you still love your wife? Are you willing to Sacrifice whatever is necessary? There is hope for your relationship. Ask her to tell you how to love her, and then do it. Ask her what she doesn't like and then stop doing it. Do the good, stop the bad and enjoy the benefits.

- Agaphilerosas, do you still want your marriage to work? Talk to him. Do not focus on the wedding so much that you miss the Sacrifices that will be needed for the marriage to succeed.

- Be willing to make physical, mental, emotional and spiritual sacrifices in order to build a Championship Relationship.

- Find out what your lover needs from you and give it to them. That is Agaphileros.

PRAYER FOR SACRIFICE

Father, _____ and _____ (we) come
before You asking You to help us to gain an
understanding of the Sacrifice that will be needed
in order for us to gain a Championship Relationship.
Help us to be prepared to make the necessary
sacrifices to win every step of the way. Grant us the
spirit of wisdom and revelation in the knowledge of
Agaphileros. Enlighten our vision so that we can
have hope, which will not make us ashamed. Show
us Your great power because we believe. Give us an
abundant supply of grace to deal with all the issues
that will come up. Give us a daily supply of strength
to face the enemies of sacrifice. Guide us with Your
word and by Your Spirit through every sacrifice. We
also ask that You grant us the rewards of sacrifice
by giving us a harvest of joy, peace and exuberant
love that surpasses anything that we have ever
seen or experienced before. Help us to draw closer

and closer together through the process of sacrifice until we become as one like You said that we should. We thank You for the victory of sacrifice, and claim it in Jesus name. Amen.

DECLARATION FOR SACRIFICE

We declare and believe that we will sacrifice everything that we must in order to fully walk in Agaphileros. We will not hold onto wrong education, experiences or advice, we will not hold forgiveness from anyone and we will establish an attitude of learning in our day to day approach to Agaphileros. We declare and believe that as we sacrifice temporary things for permanent things, there will be an explosion of Agaphileros in our relationship like never before. We declare and believe that nothing is too hard for us to do for each other because we have a permanent love that will never fade or die. We declare and believe that we will sacrifice our time, resources and energies to bring our lover into a better state and it will cause them to be totally satisfied with us. We will eat right, exercise regularly and rest accordingly for optimum ability. We declare and believe that the rewards of our sacrifices will be greater than the sacrifices themselves, even as we reap more than what we sow. We declare and believe that everything that is great comes with a great cost and we are willing to pay the cost to have a great relationship; a Championship Relationship. We will not falter, we will not fail, we will not quit, we will not give up, we will not cave in and we will not run away. Instead, we will stand, we will fight for what is great, we will sacrifice for the better life, we will make our lover the happiest person on earth and we will spare no cost to do so. We declare and believe that the sacrifice is easy because of the love that we have for each other. We give, we live, we love, we laugh, we sacrifice and we win, no matter what.

List some things that you plan to Sacrifice:

1. _____

2. _____

3. _____

4. _____

5. _____

6. _____

7. _____

8. _____

9. _____

10. _____

NOTES AND REMINDERS

MOVEMENT 3: CHANGE!

It has been said that the only constant in life is change. Of the three pillars that form a Championship Relationship "Change" is the most immediate, the most constant and the most far-reaching. It is also the one that carries the heaviest decision-making involvement. *Nothing changes until a decision is made, followed by action.* A Championship Relationship requires two decision makers. For our love to have matured and arrive at its desired destination, Jessy and I had to DECIDE to have a discussion. The discussion was needed to initiate more decisions. Real talk. Nothing changes without a decision followed by action. When we did speak, I first talked about the fact that I did not want to lose her or our marriage. Initially, it was my decision. When she spoke, one of the things that she brought up then was that she was a responder.

In other words, she was ok with my lead as long as it glorified God and she would respond to it accordingly. We were then ready to do whatever it would take. That was the beginning of Change.

You may be facing a similar situation in your marriage. If you are an Agaphilerosa and you respond to the lead of your Agaphileroso, then you may be waiting for his decision. Or maybe you are an Agaphileroso that has been previously weakened or emasculated and would prefer that your Agaphilerosa come out and take the lead. Whatever your situation, know this, until two people decide to fight for what they have there will be no Championship Relationship. Why? Because each person has a part to play in the leadership of the team. Both of you should meet to talk about it as soon as possible.

Can you imagine where the Chicago Bulls organization would have been without the decision of Michael Jordan and the Bulls ownership to go after the Championship? We probably would not even know who Scottie Pippen is. Right? An organization has to have a culture of winning. Even with a losing record they must be prepared to do whatever is necessary to win. Losing must not be a culture; it must be an obstacle on the way to being a champion. Jessy and I were not losers. We were both passionate about winning even before we were together. Some say we may have been a bit competitive. Listen! I would rather have a person on my team who is competitive and likes to win than a person who cares nothing about the game. Do you think that Scottie Pippen was upset that Michael Jordan was competitive? Do you think the owners were upset? Do you think that an organization can survive a losing mentality? Can you imagine the owner giving a speech about how they want to lose this season? NO! If you are not a loser and your spouse is not a loser, why don't you fight for what you guys have built over the years? It starts with a *decision* to fight for what you have. If you have decided that what you have is not worth fighting for, or if the other party wants to stay a loser, make up your mind that the next time you get involved in a relationship; it will be with a winner. This is not professional team sports where you get drafted into a team. This is life and you get to pick what team you want to be on. Don't lose focus on your success. You were not born to live the life of a loser. Make a winning decision today. Again, I am giving you what I believe to be good advice as I see it.

I cannot stress how important it is for both of you to be on the same page, preferably before the marriage. (Oops). Some of you have a person in your life right now that you know will not fight for the marriage or the relationship even if they get *paid* to do it. I do not believe that you are in bondage to *bondage.* You were created to be free. So be free! Stop carrying around that dead weight. (Preach Roger!) I can see some of you thanking and praising God as you read my words. (*I may not be your official counselor but I did stay at a Holiday Inn Express last night.*) lol.

Nevertheless, I am of the opinion that if God is as good as we preach, He must want me to have the best life that I can and that is what I plan to pursue. Agaphileros needs 2; an Agaphileroso and an Agaphilerosa, both going in the same direction at the same time towards the same result. I can assure you that if Jessy had not responded to my Changes in the affirmative, you would not be reading this book. There would be no Agaphileros, at least not with us.

Hallelujah to God for the decision to stay, to fight and to win! I remember how much jubilation I felt after our decision. It felt like a weight was lifted off my shoulders and I could get to work on me. I was not going to work on changing her; I was going to work on changing me. How about you? Have you made the decision to stay, to fight, and to win? Then change has begun. It is not complete but it has begun.

However, if in the process of building a Championship Relationship you notice a trait that can be devastating to what you are both building, have a conversation about it. However, be very careful how you point out faults. Jesus said something in the Gospel of Matthew that is still appropriate today for all of us. **"Why do you see the splinter that's in your brother's or sister's eye, but don't notice the log in your own eye,"** Matthew 7:3 CEB). He suggests that we take the log out of our own eyes before we can see clearly enough to take the splinter out of someone else's eye. He did not say that you cannot assist with their splinter, He just suggests that you deal with your log first. That is why Change begins with your decision to Change yourself. Be honest, because *you* are not perfect. *None of us are.* I was driving a truck full of logs into my own eyes while trying to remove a splinter from Jessy's eyes. We all have had to deal with logs. Some of us are still dealing with our logs. Logs come in many different shapes and sizes. Some logs came into our 'eyes' of our own volition and others were placed there by other people. If you still do not understand what your 'log' might be, ask an ex girlfriend, boyfriend, wife, husband, trusted friend or mentor. Ask someone who is not afraid of you and they will tell you the truth. Get a consensus. The consensus will probably be true. Decide you need to Change and then Change!

And when you are free from your own log, have a genuine conversation about their splinter. Say it with love because it's not always *what* you say that make other people upset with you, but *how* you say what you say. Do you know where I got that one from? Yes, Jessy. She told me that often until I figured it out. I had to eat a lot of humble pie when conversing with Jessy but thank God I did not have to eat for long. Take note. Be careful *how* you tell someone about *their* faults because they may be prepared to tell you about *yours.* A true love will not deliberately crush you with your faults but will try to identify them so that you can become better. That is the Log/Splinter Theory (D). So if your feelings are close to your skin then it is time to Change. Learn to drop the ego. Egos do not win Championships, rather, they destroy lives. A good friend of mine would always tell me to be humble while I was winning. Good words to live by.

One time I had gotten upset with Jessy for something even though I cannot remember why at this time. *Am I the only one that cannot remember why I got upset sometimes?* Anyway, I came home that night and she was in bed. I thought she was sleeping. She wasn't. With her back to the door, her hand lifted up out of the bed with a remote control and she pressed play on the music box. Guess what she played for me; the song that I wrote for her on our wedding day. If I had a negative ego it would not have worked. However, it did. All that I could do was smile and say how sorry I was. We had great sex that night. Everyone knows that make-up sex is one of the best types of sex (not the best though). We built our Championship Relationship that night for sure. Hehe. (Can you say "hehe" in a book?)

Agaphilerosos do not be afraid to Change. We tend to have egos, pride, selfishness and controlling attitudes; neither of which can build a Championship Relationship. I promise you that if you make the decision to let go of failure and build, you will not regret it. I didn't. You are called to be a leader. God made Adam first with intention. He never makes a mistake or wastes a creation. We have the privilege of being first. But that comes with a greater responsibility. I believe that we should get a hold of the vision first and then we can lead. There is not much that is worse than a man without a vision for the relationship that he is in. Jesus said, **"But if a blind person leads another blind person, they will both fall into a ditch."** Matthew 15:14, (CEB). Get a vision for where you are going or want to go and then be willing to lead the way. We should be the first into battle for the relationship and we should be the first to protect the relationship. We Work first, we Sacrifice first and we Change first.

We should also be the first to promote the Agaphilerosa in our lives. Never let another man promote your Agaphilerosa before you or more than you. We often say, "Ladies before gents" not because we do not want to lead, but because it is our job as the leader to give her the best. We want the world to see what a fine specimen of a lady we have, we want to put her on a pedestal and proclaim how beautiful she is, we want to open doors and take her coat and fix her chair. We feel proud as she passes by and it gives us another opportunity to see her from behind. Yes, we do look. It is so good to hold a door open for her. We get to brush up on each other as she passes by. *Unspoken words for later expectations.*

Seriously though, we must take the lead in Changing because as you lead, so goes the relationship for the most part. And if you do not Change, do not expect anything "later on" if you know what I mean. The couch is yours.

Let me also add that if your Agaphilerosa sees that you are willing to Change, it will make it so much easier for her to Change. Agaphilerosas are not the push-around walk all-over-me type. They are making more money, they are better educated and they hardly 'need' you anymore. Be willing to show that you can still lead because she needs you to. She doesn't need you to boss her around, she just needs to see you lead and grow as a leader. Some Agaphilerosas are also able to buy almost every single thing that you can give to them; they can buy their own car and a house to park the car in front of. R&B singer Ne-yo calls her, "Miss Independent." Understand where they are coming from. They are more guarded and have every reason to be because of the hurt many of them have experienced for most of their lives. Some are still working out forgiveness issues, trusting issues, independent issues, self esteem issues and more. Do not try to *make* her Change. That is not your job. Change yourself into a better man and then you can expect to be blessed by God with an Agaphilerosa that Changes as well.

Agaphilerosas, it is so essential that you release any issues that may hold you back from Change. There may be a great range of things that you have experienced. Some of you have been abused, used, tortured, forgotten, taken advantage of, and more. Yet you have survived. You have adjusted to being a single parent, a divorcee, a widow, separated and rejected. Yet you have held it together. You have *managed* it well; you have been a good steward. However, because you have had to wear both hats for so long you may be inclined to want to control everything about the relationship.

Control (D) can minimize the potential hurt that you may encounter, but it can also hurt other people. Resist that temptation and yield to Change. Control is a fear-based characteristic. Trust (D) is a faith-based characteristic. Proverbs 3:5 (CEB) says, **"Trust in the Lord with all your heart; don't rely on your own intelligence."** God created you to trust Him and be a good steward of what He gives to you; see also Proverbs 31:10-31. Manage your relationship expectations and work as a team to accomplish your goals through trust.

The one thing that I saw Jessy do over time was become more trusting of me. At first, she was uncomfortable with me coming in the bathroom if she was already in there. It sounds funny but you really haven't had a conversation until you have one while the other person is "on the throne". (Lol). Jessy was a very private lady and I could never write this series of books if she was alive. (I am telling quite a bit of our private lives to you, aren't I?) I am not so private and I love to talk, so I am working on changing that before my next Agaphilerosa shows up. I hope I am not scaring off anyone. hehehe.

It would seem to me that Agaphilerosas want to see their Agaphilerosos handle their business before placing more trust in them. Maybe that is why Churches tend to have more women than men. They have found a man called Jesus who handles his business well. If this is the case, do not be afraid to tell your Agaphileroso that you want to trust him more but you just need some time because of your past. A true Agaphileroso will not mind waiting for you and changing for you. Make sure that you give him information. Let him know what he is doing well and let him know when he may be slacking off; just tell him in a loving way. Don't delay his destiny by denying him the opportunity to make you the happiest woman in the world. Happiness has its place. Would you prefer to be happy or sad on your way to California? Talk to him, encourage him, tell him he's a stud, (I do not advocate lying, but when you are *lying down* you can speak faith). Let me give you some words to say and then you can make up your own. "Ohh baby, I love when you hold me like that. I get so wet when you kiss me. I long for your hands to squeeze my breasts. I melt when you touch me there. Take your time with me; I need you for as long as possible tonight. You make me so happy baby." Etc. And it does not have to be when having sex only. Warm him up during the day. Touch him intimately on his way out the door. Give him a long kiss before he leaves. Send him a private text. Cook his favorite meal. Tell him that the kids are spending the night with their grandparents. Tell him you need a good stud tonight. Put your underwear in his work bag. Swing by his job and sit on his lap and play with him for 10 seconds and tell him, "to be continued at home." Meet him at the garage or car port or sidewalk when he pulls up. Lead him into the house, have the place all ready, tell him he makes you so happy. He will be like a kid in a candy store so watch out for the drool from his mouth. Make sure the drool falls in the right spot, if you know what I mean.

A man loves to have his emotions caressed the right way. We are not very expressive except when challenged, motivated or aroused. Challenge him to grow your trust level. An Agaphileroso does not mind a challenge, especially if it involves his Changing into a better man for you. Motivate him to be your stud and prepare yourself accordingly. Never underestimate motivation for action. Motivation can change any man. Arouse him when you need him aroused. An Agaphileroso doesn't usually need much to get there. But teach him how to practice for the marathon. Nature breeds us for sprints but we have to be nurtured or trained for marathons. That's where you come in. (Is it me or is it getting warm in here?) I had better shift gears.

Be careful not to mistreat the Agaphileroso you have now because someone else treated you badly in the past. Do not treat Peter as if he is Paul. Every man must stand on his own merit. Remember, in Agaphileros, giving the advantage is the order of the day. Jessy helped me to Change into a leader without controlling the Change process. She learned to trust me. Her trust encouraged me to develop even more leadership skills and serve *her* at a greater level.

(I want to develop the idea of leadership a bit more extensively in Agaphileros "B" so look out for that one).

NAME SOME THINGS THAT YOU WILL CHANGE:

- _____
- _____
- _____
- _____
- _____
- _____
- _____
- _____
- _____
- _____
- _____
- _____
- _____
- _____

The list is long because you know you are both imperfect.

TAKE-AWAYS

- The only constant in life is change. Of the Three Pillars that form a Championship Relationship, "Change" is the most immediate, the most constant and the most far-reaching.

- Nothing changes until a decision is made, followed by action. A Championship Relationship requires two decision makers.

- Losing must not be a culture; it must be an obstacle on the way to being a champion.

- If you have decided that what you have is not worth fighting for, then make up your mind that the next time around, you will find someone who is a winner and go for it. Do not lose focus for your success.

- Make the decision to stay, to fight and to win. When the decision is made, change has begun.

- You were not born to live the life of a loser. Make a winning decision today.

- I am of the opinion that if God is as good as we preach, He must want me to have the best life that I can and that is what I plan to pursue.

- It's not what you say often times but how you say what you say.

- Agaphileros needs 2; an Agaphileroso and an Agaphilerosa, both going in the same direction at the same time towards the same result.

- A true love will not deliberately crush you with your faults but will try to identify them so that you can become better. Learn to drop the ego. Egos do not win Championships, rather, they destroy lives.

- Men should not be afraid to Change. We tend to have egos, pride and a selfish nature, neither of which can build a Championship Relationship. Make the decision to let go of failure and build.

- There is not much that is worse than a man without a vision for the relationship that he is in. Get a vision for where you are going or want to go and then be willing to lead the way.

- We should be the first into battle for the relationship and we should be the first to protect the relationship. We Work first, we Sacrifice first and we Change first. We should also be the first to promote the Agaphilerosa in our lives.

- Agaphilerosos, understand where Agaphilerosas are coming from. They are more guarded and have every reason to be because of the hurt many of them have experienced for most of their lives.

- Do not try to make her Change. That is not your job. Change yourself into a better man and then you can expect to be blessed by God with an Agaphilerosa that Changes as well.

- Agaphilerosas, control can minimize the potential hurt that you may encounter, but it can also hurt other people. Resist that temptation and yield to Change. Control is a fear-based characteristic. Trust is a faith-based characteristic.

- Manage your relationship expectations and work as a team to accomplish your goals through trust.

PRAYER FOR CHANGE

Father, _____ and

_____ come to You today and thank You

in advance for the Change that has begun because

of our decisions. We know that every decision has a

consequence and we are grateful for the blessings

that are coming for our good choices. Give unto us

the power of Your love and the peace of Your grace.

We humble ourselves under Your mighty hand and

ask for help in resisting the urge to walk in pride or

negative egos. Help us to be better today than we

were yesterday and better tomorrow than we are

today. We pray for the strength to keep winning

and the power to resist settling for a loss. We pray

for strength to stay, to fight and to win. Help us not

to crush one another with our words, but rather

build up each other in love, praying in the Holy

Ghost. Forgive us for falling short of success and

lead us not into temptation to fail, but deliver us

from evil. You are our shepherd so we shall not lack for love, pleasure, prosperity, health, joy, peace and change in Jesus name, Amen.

DECLARATION FOR CHANGE

We declare and believe that we are changing into the image of Agaphileros on a daily basis. Greater is he that is in us than he that is in the world. By His grace and power we change. We declare and believe that we can be much better through change and so we pursue change right now. We are becoming who we were meant to be and refuse to remain what we have become. We were meant to be great lovers and examples of true love in the earth and not people that quit, cave in and give up. We remove all excuses that can block change and declare and believe that we can be better today than we were yesterday and better tomorrow than we are today. We declare and believe that the best is yet to come in our experience and therefore we press toward the mark of the prize of the high calling of Agaphileros. We reach unto what is best and let go of the rest.

We declare and believe that we can do all things through Christ who strengthens us. We are not losers but we are winners. We declare and believe that it is our destiny to be recipients and distributors of Agaphileros because that is the way love is supposed to be. We will not settle for less. Decisions are one of our most powerful tools and we will execute good decisions that will lead us into the change that we need on a daily basis. We declare and believe that we make great decisions all the time and reap the harvest of a love of a lifetime. We will not put pressure on each other to change but rather put pressure on ourselves to be better. We declare and believe that we will see things begin to change for us right away. We call material and immaterial things to shift on our behalf; the visible and the invisible things must move in our favor and they must do it right now. We are not average lovers, we are not mediocre examples of true love and we are not going to be labeled people that are haters. We are lovers, through and through and the devil will not steal what God has promised us. We build for love, we build for life and we build for eternity. Nothing and no one can keep us from changing into the image of love, not now, not tomorrow, not ever.

NOTES AND REMINDERS

MOVEMENT 4: CONCLUSION

I was speaking to a very successful business tycoon recently and they said something very important to me. They told me that people like Oprah, Bill Gates and Warren Buffet don't go to work because they need the money like most other people. They already have more money than they can spend. These people go to work and sometimes work harder than most other people because they love what they do and they love being successful at it. Successful business people also recognize things of value and the higher the value the greater the effort they exert to obtain it. Successful people also maintain what they obtain.

May I suggest some adjustments? Learn to *love* the challenge of loving. Enjoy being a lover. Take pride in being a better lover as you get older. Older doesn't mean worse. It should mean better.

Do you think Oprah, Bill and Warren are getting worse as they get older? I do not think so. They are constantly improving, shouldn't you? Likewise, as the relationship gets older it should also get better. If you build it right you will enjoy it more and more and more.

I also recommend adjusting the value on things that are important to you so that you can produce a greater effort to obtain and maintain them. Successful people do not put stock in things of no value. Think about this. What if you wanted a successful marriage, a Championship Relationship, what would you be willing to do for it? And when you had it in your possession, what would you be willing to do to keep it? Do you want a great life where the things in your life are valuable or just an average life where values decline?

One way that you can make the person in your life a MVP (Most Valuable Player) and make yourself one as well is in the area of friendship. Friendship is really the key to value in a Championship Relationship between a man and a woman. It takes a lot of working, sacrificing and changing but the rewards are immeasurable. The level of friendship is important too. Yes, there are levels of friendships. My most important friendship for over 20 years was with the most beautiful girl in the world; Jessy. If she was here I believe that she would say the same about me; I was her most important friendship. We invested heavily in our friendship.

I'll say it like this to give you perspective. The greater the friendship the greater the value; the greater the value the greater the cost; the greater the cost the greater the reward; and the greater the reward the greater the joy. When a team wins a Championship are they sad and moping about the sports complex crying, "Woe is me"? No. They are running around spilling champagne, laughing, crying tears of joy, hugging each other, their families and everyone else. There is exuberant joy and exaltation because the Championship was obtained. I used to think that all of that celebration was so unnecessary, especially wasting good champagne, until *I* won. My friend, DO NOT LIVE LIFE WITHOUT WINNING YOUR CHAMPIONSHIP! Maybe this is all you need to hear. Maybe all that I have said up to this point was irrelevant. Don't miss this point. There is a Championship Relationship out there for you if you don't already have one. And if you have one, continue to build value into your mate and into yourself. Invest in each other constantly. Raise the value by raising the friendship level. Jessy and I had a valuable friendship and relationship and I fully intend to build an even greater Championship Relationship with the person who God blesses me with next. I am armed with information, determination and revelation to make it even better this time by building on what I had before. No one will work harder, sacrifice more or change into a better state than I will for my next wife. If I do not tell her that she is the most beautiful girl in the world all the time then I have not said anything. If she has to look to another man to meet any of her needs then I have not given anything. If she is not the happiest woman in the world every day then I have not done anything.

To the men out there that dared to read this book, I call you teammates, Agaphilerosos. We are in this together. You should have the same mindset and go after even more goals in your marriage than I will. You should be determined to build so much value in your spouses and yourself that it makes other people admire you as a couple. You should go to work on yourself every day even when you are already winning, just to keep winning; make yourself better on a daily basis. You know my mantra; *"I plan to be better today than I was yesterday, and better tomorrow than I am today."* Your kids need a great example of what they should believe God for. Your friends need a better example of how a man should treat his woman. Your woman needs to see you improving and she will follow your lead.

Your pursuit of the Championship Relationship does not end when you get married. No sir, it is enhanced. When you say I do, you are saying, "I do promise to do everything in my power to make you the happiest woman in the world, to tell you every day that I love you, to remind you that you are the most beautiful girl in the world, to let you know that I will protect the value I have placed in you and in myself and to build a Championship Relationship with you until my final breath." What woman won't fall head over heels for a man like that?

To my Agaphilerosas. You hold the key to making your man the Champion that God created him to be. Adam was incomplete without his Eve. He could not be fruitful and multiply without Eve. He could not gain his destiny without Eve. He could not be prosperous without his Eve. We need our Agaphilerosas. There is a special favor that comes with your arrival. The Bible says, "**He who finds a wife finds what is good; gaining favor from the Lord.**" Proverbs 18:22 (CEB). We are already blessed as Agaphilerosos, but we get even more favor from God because of you. He is the one who brings you to us. It is almost like God gives the man a dowry (D); a huge monetary gift, goods and real estate. This is a mystery not taught in the Body of Christ but I will briefly mention it here.

The dowry or favor only shows up when you arrive. It is because of you that marriages are so blessed. You are our prosperity, you are our Favor, You are the reason we succeed in life. Some men will never become rich without a wife from God. The dowry is provided so that the man can take care of the woman, together they can take care of the family, and the family can then take care of the community. Other cultures understand dowries more than this Western culture, but if you grab a hold of it, you will understand better why you ladies arrive with so much power. God has reserved a community blessing that can only manifest when you marry an Agaphileroso. You have power and prosperity in your hands because God is with you and He is bringing you to your Agaphileroso with a heavenly dowry. God did not design you to be a Temporary; He created you to be a Permanent. Do not settle for being a Temporary for any man.

You have the gift of vision. You see potential and you can decipher what is possible in a relatively short period of time. Proverbs 31:10-31 reveals that. *You have the gift of nurturing.* Nurture your man into greatness. I did not say to massage his ego or manipulate his efforts. Choose, rather, to nurture his T.A.G.S. If you do that to a man who is teachable, you are well on your way to being happy. *You have the gift of helps and you are a master of resources.* Jessy always had resources tucked away somewhere to help in a time of need. Use every available resource that you can put your hands on to *understand* how a man thinks and then approach him with wisdom. You can do it and he is depending on you.

I am telling you the truth, I was nothing without Jessy. "Agaphileros" is a dowry that God brought to me all those years ago. I am just now seeing it. It was wrapped in a lot of challenges and obstacles but I can see clearly now that the rain (pain) has gone. When Jessy found me my heart was broken and I was all messed up. She took my heart, mended it, fixed it up real good and made it better than it was before, and before she died she gave it back to me so that one day I could give it to someone else who would deserve it. Not a Temporary, but a Permanent from God. *And* one day, because of Jessy, my next Agaphilerosa and I will experience Agaphileros; love the way it is supposed to be, forever! Thank you Jessy and baby I will always love you.

MOVEMENT 5: EXTRAS!

DICTIONARY

Agaphileros - Love, the way it is supposed to be.

Agaphilerosa - A female that walks in Agaphileros.

Agaphilerosas - Women that walk in Agaphileros.

Agaphileroso - A male that walks in Agaphileros.

Agaphilerosos - Men that walk in Agaphileros.

Championship Relationship - It is a relationship wherein two people win every time, no matter what.

Change - The most immediate and far-reaching thing that you can do to win. It is moving from one mindset to another.

Control - To exercise restraint or direction over; dominate; command; to eliminate or prevent the flourishing or spread of. (Dictionary.com)

Dowry - The money, goods or estate that a wife brings to her husband at marriage. (Dictionary.com)

Ego - The "I" or self of any person. Egotism; conceit, self importance. Self-esteem or self image. (Dictionary.com)

Emasculating - Making a man feel like he is not a man to you. You can do this by telling him that he cannot satisfy you, or saying something about his performance or disregarding the things he does as a man. **Choose education over emasculation.**

Log/Splinter Theory - Jesus' discourse in Matthew 7:3 about removing the log out of your own eye before you try to remove the splinter out of someone else's eye. Deal with your faults before trying to deal with other people's faults.

Manage - To bring about or succeed in accomplishing, sometimes despite difficulty or hardship. (Dictionary.com)

Manipulate - To manage or influence skillfully, especially in an unfair manner. (Dictionary.com)

Mind-Set - Your education, experiences and influence. These make up your mind-set or how you set your mind. Your education comes from a teacher in some formal setting. Your experiences come from life's journey. Your influences are those people and things that can impact your decision making process.

Movement - A sequence of thoughts in a section. Movements cause adjustments.

Permanent Purpose - It is when God has given you the plans that He has for you and those plans will not change.

Rogerisms - Sayings, writings and poetic words made up by Roger A. Watson, Mr. Triple L.

Sacrifice - The price you will have to pay to have real success.

T.A.G.S. - Talents, Abilities, Gifts and Skills. These are the things that you love to do and would not mind doing for the rest of your life. You find them exhilarating.

Temporary Pleasure - Someone or something that is not meant to be permanent in your life and may cost you more than you thought. It may also keep you from your Permanent Purpose.

Temporary Purpose - A job, career, path, business or venture that is not meant to be permanent in your life and may cost you more than you planned to pay. It may also keep you from your Permanent Purpose.

Three pillars - Work, Sacrifice and Change. They are the three pillars in a Championship Relationship.

Trust - To be confident, bold, sure, put hope in, to put refuge in. (Strong's Concordance, Hebrew)

Work - Doing the simple things to the best of your ability and doing it all the time.

WHAT AN AGAPHILEROSA SHOULD PRAY

Father, I come to You in the name of Jesus, thanking you for the men in my life. I thank you first of all for the elders in my family and in my life. I honor them and ask that Your hand of blessing will be upon them as they navigate their lives on a daily basis. I pray that all the men in my life live under an open heaven, walk over a closed hell and that no weapon of the enemy will stop their purpose.

Give the man for my life, my Agaphileroso, an anointing to love me in such a way that I will always be satisfied with his love. I pray that you and I will teach him how to love me like I have never been loved before. Let him be my lover to his last breath. Help him to treat me the way that I was created to be treated. Give him what he needs to be my best friend and cause him to always make me happy.

Give him wisdom and show him how to cherish me and support me like he has never cherished or supported anyone before. Make him my greatest fan and biggest cheerleader. Let him be a life-long learner, and give him the understanding to know what I like and do not like; what I want and do not want. Give me an Agaphileroso that will perform whatever I need, whenever I need it and wherever I need it. Yes Lord! Bless me with a lover that will put me first in our relationship and never disrespect me. Let him be a lover that will be kind and gentle to me at all times. Help him to never embarrass me for as long as I live. Bless me with a king that will appreciate all that I do and that will treat me like the queen that I am. Let him be a husband that will be willing to give his life for me as Jesus did for the church, a man that will not hesitate to give me the advantage and who would love me unconditionally at all times. Let him be everything that I want and need in every area of my life. And help me to become all that he needs and wants. Bless our union and make it an example of the power of love. These requests I submit to You today in Jesus name.

Now make a list of the qualities that you are looking for in an Agaphileroso.

1. _____

2. _____

3. _____

4. _____

5. _____

6. _____

7. _____

8. _____

9. _____

10. _____

11. _____

12. _____

13. _____

14. _____

15. _____

WHAT AN AGAPHILEROSO SHOULD PRAY

Father, I come to You in the name of Jesus and I thank You for the life that You have given to me. I ask that You will bless all the women in my life who are still alive that have looked after me and cared for me. I especially ask that You will bless my Agaphilerosa. I ask that You help me to cherish her and love her like Christ loved the Church and gave Himself for it. Make me more teachable. Teach me daily what it means to give myself to You and give myself for her. Show me the full spectrum of Agaphileros every day of my life so that I will not be a failure but a success. Teach me the difference between what is Permanent and what is Temporary so that I do not give up what is Permanent for what is Temporary. Help me to stand as a man for what is right and what is eternal. I want to be the Protector of my family. I want to be the Provider for my family. I want to be the Leader for my family. And I want You to show me how to do these things. As I am being Changed into an Agaphileroso, I ask that You will prepare for me a love of a lifetime, a one of a kind woman that will be everything that I want and everything that I need and desire. Give me someone with the external and internal qualities that will always make me excited to be her lover and her husband. Fill her with all the managerial skills that I need to bring out the best in me. Give me an Agaphilerosa that will not destroy or crush me but one that will help me to grow as a man. Someone that can build trust with me and me with her. Someone that is able to communicate to me what her needs are and then I will trust You to help me and equip me to meet those needs. Help me to love her walk, her talk, her smile, her laugh, her mind and her ways. Teach me how to make love to her soul, her mind, her spirit and her body. Make me an all rounder where she is concerned. Give me an Agaphilerosa that can make me the happiest man in the world. Protect me from a woman of drama and mess, a woman who wants to hurt me and destroy me, a woman that will mess up my Permanent Purpose and end my destiny. Deliver her from her past and all the men that have hurt her whether they were family or friends, boyfriends or husbands. Deliver her from seeking her own advantage as You also deliver me from seeking my own. Deliver her from any negative qualities that she may have that are like Eve, Delilah and Jezebel. Give her good qualities that are good and healthy like Mary, Rebekah and Sarah. Father, I seek an Agaphilerosa with a Championship mindset, one of elevated thinking, a woman that is going to the same destination as I am. And as we get together, help me to listen and respond to her needs more than my own. Help me to love her in ways that she has never been loved before. Help me to make her the happiest woman in the world on a daily basis. Help me to never make her jealous about another woman for as long as we may live. Help me to be the support that she needs to become all that she can be in You and arrive at her God-given destination on time. I need Your help every moment of my life to be ready to love at the highest level that I have ever loved at before. I commit my life to You to be fully equipped for her only, and I vow to fulfill my duties to her until my last breath, in Jesus name, Amen.

Now make a list of the qualities that you are looking for in an Agaphilerosa.

1. _____

2. _____

3. _____

4. _____

5. _____

6. _____

7. _____

8. _____

9. _____

10. _____

11. _____

12. _____

13. _____

14. _____

15. _____

16. _____

THE VOW

(for two to say together)

I _____ vow to love you

_____and I _____ vow

to love you _____ also, for the rest of

our lives together. I vow to love you without

restrictions and limitations of expression and

display. I vow to love you until the clock runs out of

time, till the end of the line, because forever you'll

be mine. I vow to hold you until the winter ceases

to come and until the last day of the sun. I vow to

make you the only person I will ever long for in this

life, the only person that I will ever need to satisfy

me, the only one I desire. I vow to be your best

friend and I will not put anyone ahead of you. I vow

to tell you everything and I will always tell you the

truth, even if it makes me look bad. I vow to never

hurt you with the things I say, or with the things I

do. I vow to speak to you in a caring and thoughtful

manner and never put you down. I vow to be appreciative and thankful for all that you do and never take you for granted. I vow to lift you up and promote you into what God has called you to do. I will support your endeavors and be considerate of your efforts. I vow to protect you from people and things that will hurt you and I will always have your back. I vow to protect our home and I will not allow anything to destroy what we have built. I vow to protect our family at all cost and I will utilize all my resources to do so. I vow to cherish you, honor you, bless you, love you and keep you in the one and only spot in my heart. I vow you my love, my heart and my body until my last breath.

Your Agaphileroso

Your Agaphilerosa

Add some vows of your own

1. _____

2. _____

3. _____

4. _____

5. _____

6. _____

7. _____

MOVEMENT 6: ROGERISMS

AGAPHILEROS ACRONYMS

Here are some acronyms to start you off. It is really sexy to have code words or signs between lovers or lovers to be. Make up some of your own. Have fun with it.

BBF	Best Bestest Friend
BBFF	Best Bestest Friend Forever
CAGWM	Come And Go With Me
FLY	Forever Loving You
IHSFU	I Have Something For You
IWAMWYT	I Want A Marathon With You Tonight
IWBYST	I Will Be Your Stud Tonight
IWMST	I Want My Stud Tonight
IWNSLU	I Will Never Stop Loving U
IWTBAWU	I Want To Be Alone With U

IYFL	I'm Your Forever Love
JTTOU	Just The Two Of Us
LTAS	Let's Take A Shower
LTAV	Let's Take A Vacation
MILWY	Madly In Love With You
MONEAO	My ONE And Only
MUSM	Miss U So Much
NGLUG	Never Gonna Let U Go
OLIF	Our Love Is Forever
OLWLF	Our Love Will Last Forever
TBY	Thinking 'Bout You
TUFAC	Thank You For Another Chance
UAITF	U Are Impossible To Forget
WIWT	Wish I Was There
WUWH	Wish You Were Here
YAAA	You Are Absolutely Amazing

Now make up some of your own. Remember, it can be anything and no one has to know what it means but both of you.

_____   _____

_____   _____

_____   _____

_____   _____

_____   _____

_____   _____

_____   _____

_____   _____

_____   _____

ALL I EVER WANTED WAS YOU

(In case your Agaphilerosa is missing)

You have painted your love on my heart, the canvas
of my heart

And now you're not here, my world is falling apart

All I ever wanted was you, all I ever needed was you

You can ask God if it's true, all my desire is for you

And at night, I just know that it's not right, when I
turn down the light

And you, you're my bride, but not by my side

And please don't stay, don't stay away come what
may

For I need you here, I need you here today

I long for, I live for, to hold you

I want to, I need to, be with you

Desire, Aspire, to fire

The flame of your love burning me

SPANISH LOVE WORDS

(from Jah Cure's "Unconditional Love". Never know when this may come in handy.)

El amor es puro: The love is pure

Quiero amarte para siempre: I want to love you forever

Enseñame como amarte incondicionalmente: Teach me how to love unconditionally

No necesito nada: I don't need anything

Ni a nadie: Nothing and nobody

Si te tendo aquí: If I have you here

Te amo para siempre: I love you forever

Te amo eternamente: I love you for eternity

Tú me enseñaste como amar: You taught me how to love

Y por eso te agradezco: And so I thank you

Te amo mi amor: I love you my love

Y te voy a amar incondicionalmente: And I will love you unconditionally

Amo...Mi amor: Love...My Love

KISS

(newly weds temporarily apart from each other)

Yes I said KISS, for me it was all Bliss, it's what I really really Miss, as I fall into this Abyss,

An abyss of love so True, memories rushing Through, a love just for Two, falling head over heels for You,

Falling is my new Theme, giving up the old Schemes, releasing inhibited Dreams, flowing in Streams,

Streams of Water, that tastes so Bitter, without my Lover, so please Remember,

Remember our first Kiss, and also This, my dear sweet Miss, hear me in This,

As we begin this Trip, my fingers in your finger Tips, my hips touching your Hips, lips to Lips,

Kissing with Passion, the world in Oblivion, love in Resurrection, right Direction,

Kiss me once More, before you walk out the Door, kiss me once More, that's what lips are For.

SO UNFAIR!

(for if she is just that fine that no other woman can compare)

I thought about something, while I was typing, that life has some happenings that are worth mentioning.

Why in the world, would God make a girl, which was able to curl, my heart like a twirl.

It is SO UNFAIR, and yes I dare, to boldly declare, no way would I share.

The deepness of the eyes, the smoothness of the thighs, a heart with no lies, a voice that gets me high.

A neck so slender, a brain so super, a waistline bender, moves it like a blender.

Hands to touch me, Lips to kiss me, Ears to hear me, a lover to keep me.

And after all is said and done, looking from the top to the ground, and turning around and around, she won, hands down.

So have no fear, look at her right there, God took great care, to make her SO UNFAIR.

WINNING!

(for when you have a powerful woman)

It's a constant theme of her life

It's what she speaks every night

And as she wakes in the morning

It's on her lips as she gets going

She is a winner and has no failure

She wins, and that couldn't be clearer

Don't look for her in the gutter

Because she always soars higher

She can give you a good job

As long as you aren't a slob

Her pockets are full of money

Her words flow like honey

(Continued on next page)

You can't be her friend like so

Just because you got some dough

She doesn't win with your stuff

And she won't take your foolish fluff

You had better come real good

Whether from the penthouse or the hood

This is Mrs. Independent for sure

So losers take a detour

What are some things you can identify that make your woman a WINNER?

1. _____

2. _____

3. _____

4. _____

5. _____

6. _____

YOU HAD ME AT HELLO

(for those who loved at first sight or first word)

I'm not sure if I ever mentioned to you before

But baby girl you are the only one I adore

You have all of me and I beg, never let me go

Because Baby girl, you had me at hello

I'm not sure if I told you the secret to my heart

But you sealed the deal right from the start

Just your presence is enough for my show

Because Baby girl, you had me at hello

I'm not sure if I mentioned how you're so amazing

But when I'm with you I just go to praising

I pray that our love will continue to grow

Because Baby girl, you had me at hello

(Continued on next page)

I'm not sure if I mentioned that all others are gone

Gone like the objects of some sad love song

You're all I ever wanted and I love you so

Because Baby girl, you had me at hello

I'm not sure if love can be any greater than this

'Cause when you're not here, it's you that I miss

So as long as I live I'll never let you go

Because Baby girl, you had me at hello

What are some of the first things you can recall about her that sparked your interest?

1. _____

2. _____

3. _____

4. _____

I THOUGHT ABOUT YOU

(if you are not married yet but think about her ALL the time)

I was on a plane listening to music and I thought about you

I was flying high in comfort next to a model and I thought about you

I looked at her and said to myself, not bad but nothing like you

I wished you were right here next to me as I was thinking about you

I landed in another city and guess what, I thought about you

I was having fun with my friends and I thought about you

I wondered what you might be doing as I thought about you

I prayed that you'd be safe and sound as I thought about you

(Continued on next page)

I got on another plane and yes, there I was, thinking about you

I saw this beautiful elderly couple and I thought about you

I wondered if we would get old together as I thought about you

I wished that it was God's will for us as I thought about you

I came to my empty home and stood there thinking about you

I turned the key, walked in and I was thinking about you

I began to wonder what it'd be like to walk in and see you

And not have to spend so much time only thinking about you

Write some notes here on what you have thought about doing with her and to her and for her. Then hide this book from all eyes except the both of you. Refer to it from time to time to make sure the list is completed. Repeat!

1. _____

2. _____

3. _____

4. _____

5. _____

6. _____

7. _____

8. _____

9. _____

10. _____

DANCE

(not bad for a wedding night)

Can I dance with you the rest of my life

Can I shout thank God that you're my wife

Can I touch you there yes right there too

Can I hold you close with lover's glue

Can I dance with you for the rest of time

Can I feel your soft cheek next to mine

Can I touch your shoulders soft to touch

Can I whisper how I need you so much

Can I dance with you and you with me

Can I make you see what I see

Can I tell you how you move so fine

Can I tell you how I'm glad you're mine.

YOU INSPIRE ME...

(read this one to her if she inspires you)

I feel inspired. You Inspire me so I write.

I feel happy. You Inspire me so I sing.

I feel at peace. You Inspire me so I am calm.

I feel like falling. You Inspire me so I trust.

I feel closer. You Inspire me to hold.

I feel taller. You Inspire me to reach.

I feel humble. You Inspire me to bow.

I feel like staying. You Inspire me to wait.

I feel alive. You Inspire me to live.

I feel insane. You Inspire me to be crazy.

I feel satisfied. You Inspire me to share.

I feel like giving. You Inspire me to love.

WE WIN!

(if you know that together you are winners no matter what)

In spite of the obstacles, the hurt and many spectacles

Don't you know we were created to WIN?

The long and dark nights, the arguments and the fights

Don't you know we were created to WIN?

The mistakes, the sorry's, and the forgive me's

Don't you know we were created to WIN?

The broken friendships, loose lips and sunken ships

Don't you know we were created to WIN?

(Continued on next page)

The money that was lost, how we counted up the cost

Don't you know we were created to WIN?

The many prayers and fasting, the desires and the asking

Don't you know we were created to WIN?

So together we will be, together you and me

And I'll tell you again, WE WIN!

WAITING ON ONE

(if you were together, broke up, and now are

waiting on each other to become 'ready' again)

Have you ever had to wait on something that you
expected to come to you?

And at the end of the day you were still without it
and that made you blue.

Have you ever had to wait on someone that you
expected to show?

But in the end they didn't, and away you had to go.

But if you ever have to wait for the ONE you will
never be sad

Cause every time they speak, their voice makes you
glad

They always bring sunshine to your rainiest of days

And for their friendship you always give God praise

(Continued on next page)

I know someONE like that and I have been waiting
for a long time

To bring sunshine into their toughest of days and do
it full time

I wish to bless them when in the morning they wake

And put them back together if they ever break.

If you should ever come across her path do this one
thing for me

Let her know I'm ok and I am as happy as I can be

Because she sought me out when she did not have
to

And took away my dark clouds and made my sky
blue

Tell her for me that I don't mind waiting on ONE

Cause that's all that I need and after that I'm done

No others left on earth for me; I'm out of the game

No room left in my heart for another to claim.

I WISH!

(for those who let the right one go and are hopeful

for a Second Time Around with them. Cue Shalamar)

I wish that I could retrace my steps

I wish that I could start over again

I wish that the lies would have been true

I wish that the truth would have been you

I wish that I could have said sorry

I wish that I could have shut my mouth

I wish that you would have stayed

I wish that my debt was paid

(Continued on next page)

I wish that I would have had more understanding

I wish that I would have made you understand

I wish that my reality was only you

I wish that all my dreams were true

I wish that I could be a better man

I wish that I could be your only plan

I wish that our time was eternity

I wish that our love flowed endlessly

I wish above all for your happiness

I wish for you God's very best

I wish that all your dreams come through

And I wish to share them all with you

What are some things that you would have done differently or what did you learn from letting her or him go?

1. _____
2. _____
3. _____
4. _____
5. _____
6. _____
7. _____

YOU MAKE ME HOT HOT HOT!

(Get the water hose)

Baby I was thinking about you and what you got

I want you to know, I started feeling *hot hot hot*

The way you walk and talk, to me is so doggone good

Makes me want to love you like no one else ever could

Your smile is intoxicating, your laugh exhilarating

You start my muscles to moving my rocket to launching

And when you call my name you send chills up my spine

When I am uptight, you alone can help me unwind

You got me so hot sweetness that I'm on fire

You make me pull out my pistol, my gun for hire

You're blazing such a trail of heat in my bones

So I got you a heat seeking missile for when we're alone.

(continued from previous page)

I'm gonna blow you up, make you scream, sing and shout

Until you see and feel what this heat is all about

And as we make extreme love I'll be the fire to your pot

Bring you to the boiling point and make you *hot hot hot.*

ONE WORD, 50 TIMES

(forget the water hose)

1.   Celestial. Absolute. Total. Complete. Abundant. Strong. Admirable. Fit. Excellent. Comely. Cute. Pleasing. Pretty. Magnificent. Superior. Royal. Lovely. Ideal. Marvelous. Symmetrical. Tasteful, Well. Stunning. Gorgeous. Alluring. Superb. Elegant. Refined. Luxurious, Ravishing. Appealing. Nice. Delicate. Graceful. Beautiful. Attractive. Classy. Angelic. Wonderful. Pulchritudinous. Charming. Bright. Radiant. Awesome. Dazzling. Glorious. Splendid. Remarkable. Divine.

2.   Wise. Smart. Servant. Sharp. Spectacular. Witty. Creative. Ingenious. Genius. Bright. Ready. Resourceful. Sassy. Adept. Alert. Whiz. Bold. Brainy. Brilliant. Knowledgeable. Informed. Intelligent.

(continued from previous page)

Scholarly. Nimble. Quick. Shrewd. Effective.

Consistent. Efficient. Proficient. Producer. Prudent.

Investor. Manager. Ability. Astute. Discerning.

Exceptional. Reasonable. Aware. Understanding.

Sound. Sensible. Perceptive. Judicious. Educated.

Experienced. Discreet. Contemplative. Original.

3.	Hot. Sexy. Arousing. Cuddly. Loving.

Affectionate. Voluptuous. Steamy. Spicy. Mature.

Provocative. Radiant. Racy. Seductive. Sensual.

Sensitive. Flirtatious. Inviting. Crazy. Adventurous.

Exciting. Private. Erotic. Passionate. Romantic.

Kissable. Aphrodisiac. Tender. Precious. Enamored.

Enchanting. Appealing. Pleasing. Titillating. Teasing.

Delightful. Glamorous. Ravishing. Gratifying.

Pleasurable. Libidinous. Suggestive. Penetrating.

Enticing. Lovely. Desirous. Bootylicious. Vibrant.

Soft. Perfect.

(continued from previous page)

4.   Talk. Listen. Brush. Look. Touch. Feel. Kiss. Brave. Remember. Hold. Off. Scatter. Lay. Close. Move. Tongue. Yes. Please. Start. Pleasure. Scream. Plead. Beg. Stop? No! Start. Again. Work. Up. Down. Around. Between. Two. One. In. Out. Rise. Flat. Twist. Turn. Moan. Groan. Pleased. Happy. Twice. Happier. Creative. Joy. Satisfied. Repeat.

AAAAAAAAAAHHHHHHHHHH!!!!!

Let us close off this book of writings so that you can do whatever you need to do. Contact your spouse if they are not with you right now. It's time. Set the mood for the time and place that you are in. Whatever floats your boat; candles, food, fruit, wine, bubble bath, music, kids to friends house, movie, whatever. Wherever you may not have been in a while; bedroom, bathroom, kitchen, dining room, attic, basement, by the fireplace, on the table, in the backyard, by the pool, in the pool, in the shed, in the car, on the car.

Agaphilerosos, read the last two Rogerisms again but try facing her this time. Look into her eyes after every word and line. Be ready to flow together in whatever way you feel it and think it. Begin to use *every* love tool God blessed you with. Enjoy. AGAPHILEROS!

REFERENCES

All Scripture references and inspirations where noted are from The Amplified Bible and The Common English Bible.

Scripture quotations taken from The Amplified® Bible, Copyright © 1954, 1958, 1962, 1964, 1965, 1987 by the Lockman Foundation. Used by permission. (www.Lockman.org).

The Common English Bible, Copyright © 2011. The Christian Resources Development Corporation. Nashville, TN.

www.dictionary.com (2013). Retrieved May 1st, 2013.

THE BEGINNING!

Join the Agaphileros Experience at www.facebook.com/agaphileros or text us at 678-321-RAW1 (7291) to get on the text list or call us at 206-279-1624 or send me an email at rogerwatson888@hotmail.com to join the email list. You can also go to www.agaphileros.com (under construction) or www.icg.yolasite.com for ordering information. Let me know what you would like me to talk about in future books in the "Agaphileros" series. I am already working on the next one so let me hear from you.

Send your comments or requests to: rogerwatson888@hotmail.com. For booking information call 206-279-1624 and leave a detailed message. If you enjoyed it, spread the word and help us to reach our goal of creating more Agaphilerosos and Agaphilerosas in this country and around the world. Thank you.

UPCOMING TOPICS FOR AGAPHILEROS "B" DUE FEB 14, 2014.

(Subject to change)

- Forgiveness and Mercy levels.
- Divorce, Death and Dominion.
- The Abuse Family.
- How to be all the man that she desires.
- How to be the entire woman that he desires.
- Promise, Pain and Purpose.
- Questionnaire: What questions should you ask before you say I do?
- Giving the Advantage.
- Your 3 Main commodities; time, resources and energy.
- Leadership in a Championship Relationship.

www.ingramcontent.com/pod-product-compliance
Lightning Source LLC
Chambersburg PA
CBHW050124280326
41933CB00010B/1239